# Easy Spicy Fish Recipes and Recipe Workbook

Spicy Fish Recipes For You to Try And A Workbook to Keep Note Of Your Cooking Experiments. Companion Book To Easy Spicy Fish

Joseph Veebe

*This Recipe Book and Journal Belongs To*

-----------------------------------------------

**Copyright © 2020 by Joseph Veebe. All Rights Reserved.**

No part of this publication may be reproduced, distributed, or transmitted in any form or by any means, including photocopying, recording, or other electronic or mechanical methods, or by any information storage and retrieval system without the prior written permission of the publisher, except in the case of very brief quotations embodied in critical reviews and certain other noncommercial uses permitted by copyright law.

# Other Books in this Series:

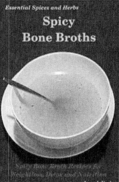

# EASY SPICY FISH – RECIPES AND RECIPE WORKBOOK

## TABLE OF CONTENTS

Table of Contents ............................................................................................................. 4
    Introduction ................................................................................................................ 6
    Health Benefits of Spices ........................................................................................... 6
    Nutritional Profile of Fish ......................................................................................... 6
    Healthy Fish Tips ....................................................................................................... 7
    Notes on Recipes in this book ................................................................................... 8
**Chapter 1. Baked, Grilled, and Fried Fish** ................................................................. 10
    Fish Fry .................................................................................................................... 10
    Baked Fish in Yogurt Sauce ..................................................................................... 12
    Tandoori Salmon ..................................................................................................... 14
    15 Minute Spicy Fish Fry ........................................................................................ 16
    Spicy Fish in Banana Leaf ...................................................................................... 18
    Spicy Grilled Fish .................................................................................................... 22
**Chapter 2. Spicy Curried Fish** ..................................................................................... 25
    10 Minute Salmon Curry ......................................................................................... 25
    Salmon with Green Mango ...................................................................................... 28
    Spicy Pickled Fish ................................................................................................... 30
    Recipes Using Canned Fish .................................................................................... 34
    Quick Canned Sardine Masala ................................................................................ 34
    Quick Fish Curry With Canned Tuna ..................................................................... 36
    Goan Fish Curry ...................................................................................................... 38
    Fish Makhani .......................................................................................................... 42
    Fish in Yogurt Sauce ............................................................................................... 44
    Chettinadu Fish Curry ............................................................................................. 46
    Malabar Fish Curry ................................................................................................. 50
    Coconut Milk Fish Curry ........................................................................................ 54
    Kerala Fish Curry .................................................................................................... 56
    Mangalore Fish Curry ............................................................................................. 58
    Turmeric Fish .......................................................................................................... 60
**Chapter 3. International Spicy Fish Recipes** ............................................................. 62
    Seafood Paella ......................................................................................................... 62
    Spicy Korean Fish Stew .......................................................................................... 64
    Spicy Mediterranean Shakshuka Fish #1 ................................................................ 66
    Spicy Mediterranean Shakshuka Fish #2 ................................................................ 68

- Spicy Fish with Kimchi ................................................................................................ 70
- Fish in Creamy Cajun Sauce ........................................................................................ 72
- Sweet and Spicy Brazilian Fish Stew ........................................................................... 74
- Instant Pot Spicy Spanish Seafood Stew ...................................................................... 78
- Spicy Herb Baked Fish ................................................................................................. 80
- Spicy Mediterranean Baked Fish .................................................................................. 82
- Sri Lankan Fish Curry .................................................................................................. 84
- Spicy Salmon with Coconut Sauce ............................................................................... 88
- Easy Thai Red Curry with Fish .................................................................................... 90
- Spicy Mediterranean-Indian-Thai Fish ......................................................................... 92
- Spicy Louisiana Fish Fry .............................................................................................. 94
- Spicy Grilled Fish in Coconut Sauce (Samaki Wa Kupaka) ........................................ 96

Final Notes and General Tips for Cooking Spicy Fish ......................................................100

Disclaimer ..........................................................................................................................109

Cooking Measurements and Conversion Charts .................................................................110

# EASY SPICY FISH – RECIPES AND RECIPE WORKBOOK

## INTRODUCTION

This is the 4th book on the "Easy Spicy Recipes" series. As explained in the previous books, spices and herbs have a long and proven history of effective use as a flavoring ingredient in food preparations as well as medicinal use in potions, tinctures, and other alternative therapies.

Fish is one of the easiest and fastest proteins to cook. It can be boiled, steamed, roasted, fried, sautéed, curried, baked, grilled, or barbequed in 10 minutes or less.

The recipes in the book combine the natural goodness of fish with the medicinal and healing properties of spices and herbs and create wholesome, healthy, anti-inflammatory, and disease-fighting recipe ideas.

The recipes in the book are put together so they can be easily prepared using ingredients that are natural, healthy, and commonly available. There are several optional ingredients that you can try out to make the dish according to your taste and creativity. Most recipes follow a set of notes which give ideas to tweak the recipe to your liking.

This book contains primarily fish preparations that are spicy and using common spices and herbs. Fish recipes that do not use spices are not part of this book.

While the author loves cooking for his family, he does not like to follow a strict prescription or rigid recipes. He believes in spending as little time in the kitchen as possible while preparing natural, healthy, and tasty food. He likes to be creative and try out various ingredients also do not follow strict measurements.

## HEALTH BENEFITS OF SPICES

Spices and herbs used in recipes described in this book have many health benefits. Some of them are listed below.
- Antioxidant properties
- Anti-inflammatory properties
- Anti-cancer properties
- Anti-fungal, anti-microbial, anti-viral
- Help the immune system and fight infections.
- Lower blood pressure
- Lower cholesterol
- Lower diabetes
- Improve circulation.

Spices and herbs, if used correctly, could improve overall health, and help fight many health conditions in a natural and supplemental fashion to modern treatments.

## NUTRITIONAL PROFILE OF FISH

Fish is one of the healthiest foods. Fish is low-fat, high protein, and packed with omega-3 fatty acids and vitamins such as vitamin D and B2 (riboflavin). Also, fish contains calcium, iron, zinc, magnesium, iodine, and potassium.

Omega-3 fatty acids (EPA (eicosapentaenoic acid) and DHA (docosahexaenoic acid)) found in fish are essential nutrients that keep our heart and brain healthy. Our bodies do not generate these nutrients and therefore we must eat foods that are high in them such as fish, nuts, and eggs. Fatty fishes such as salmon, sardines, mackerel, trout, and herring are especially good. Because fish is a lean protein, it is a good choice if you are on a weight loss diet.

170 grams (6 oz) of fish typically provide the following (the figures are approximate and depend on the type of fish):
- 39 grams of protein
- 22 grams of fat
- 200 calories
- 1-2g of omega-3 fatty acids
- 112 mg of cholesterol
- 650 mg of potassium
- 100 mg of sodium
- Good source of vitamin A, vitamin B-6, calcium, and magnesium

## HEALTHY FISH TIPS

While freshly cooked fish is a good healthy food choice, pre-prepared fish such as breaded fish, fish sticks, fish sandwich (made of breaded fish) does not necessarily provide the same benefits. They may have higher calories, fat, and sugar.

Fish can also be contaminated, and some fish may have higher levels of mercury. Here are some of the fishes with low levels of mercury. Estimates are based on 170 grams (6 oz.) filet of fish and are given in parts per billion (ppb):
- Bass (240 ppb)
- Catfish (280 ppb)
- Clams, Oysters (40-50 ppb)
- Cod (140 ppb)
- Crawfish (70 ppb)
- Salmon (50 ppb)
- Sardines (150 ppb)
- Tilapia (50 ppb)
- Squid, scallops, Shrimp (80-100 ppb)
- Lobster (400 ppb)

Fishes with higher levels of mercury:
- Swordfish (1800 ppb)
- Spanish Mackerel (900 ppb)
- Grouper (800 ppb)
- Trout (700 ppb)
- Snapper, Tuna, Halibut (450-550 ppb)

This information is included just so that you are aware of which fish has more mercury levels than others. FDA/EPA guidelines for eating fish is given below in the chart (source US FDA). If you are pregnant or nursing, you may want to stick to the best choice of fish.

If you, like me, are the one who is doing the shopping, you want to make informed choices before buying fish such as:
- When was the fish caught? Usually, fish tastes better within the first 4 days of being caught.
- How does it look/smell? If there is a bad smell, likely it is not fresh. If you look at their gills and see that they start to discolor, it means it is about to go bad.
- Where it is from. Certainly, wild-caught fish is better than farmed fish as farmed fish may be raised using hormones and/or antibiotics.

## NOTES ON RECIPES IN THIS BOOK

Recipes in this book are not a collection of authentic dishes, but a spicy version of fish recipes that are easy to make and 100% healthy and flavorful. Ingredients used are mostly natural without any preserved or processed foods. Most of these recipes include tips and tricks to vary and adapt to your taste as well as your tolerance of spice levels. You can also substitute ingredients you like and skip the ones you don't like.

There are about 40 recipes in the book with ideas to make another 40 or even more with the suggestions and notes included with many of the recipes. Cooking does not have to be prescriptive but can be creative. If you are like me who does not want to spend a lot of time in the kitchen but love to cook healthy, natural, and wholesome food, this book is for you. I invite you to try your own variations and apply your creativity to cook dishes that are truly your own. Please see my book "Beginner's Guide to Cooking with Spices" to find out many health benefits of individual spices and tips and tricks in using them.

Notes:

## CHAPTER 1. BAKED, GRILLED, AND FRIED FISH

Fish cooks fast and can be fried, baked, or grilled in 10-15 minutes or less. Fish marinated in spice paste may be fried in oil, baked, broiled, or grilled. If you are using whole fish, clean it first (scales and or skin removed), make cuts into the fish and apply the spice marinade before cooking.

### FISH FRY

Below is a recipe for fish steak marinated with spices and then shallow fried. This could be eaten as an appetizer or served with rice. Fish steaks with bones removed or fishes with larger or easy to remove bones are ideal. Salmon, Tilapia, catfish filets, pomfret, or kingfish may be used.

**Ingredients**
- 1 lb. fish steaks
- 2-3 tsp chili powder
- ½ tsp black pepper powder
- ½ tsp turmeric powder
- 1 tbsp ginger garlic paste
- 2 tsp lime juice
- ½ cup oil to fry

Method
1. Combine all the spices powders, salt, ginger garlic paste, and make a paste. Add 1 tbsp water if required.
2. Pat the fish pieces dry with a napkin. If you are using whole fish or fish steaks, make shallow cut marks on the fish pieces so that spice mix can get into the fish.
3. Apply the masala paste and rub it into the fish, especially into the cut marks. Set aside for a couple of hours or at least 30 minutes to marinate.
4. Heat coconut oil in a flat pan on medium heat. Shallow fry on both sides of the fish for 2-3 minutes or until done.
5. Remove fish from the pan. Apply the lime juice on top of the fish and serve with rice.

## My Recipe Notes

**Result:** Loved it ♥   Okay ☑   Not for me ☒
**Spice Level:** Too Spicy 😊   Just Right ☺   Not Spicy Enough 😎
**Date(s):**
**Comments:**

## BAKED FISH IN YOGURT SAUCE

Ingredients
- 4-6 pieces of salmon filet
- 2 tsp turmeric powder
- ½ tsp pepper powder (optional)
- ½ -1 tsp chili powder (optional)
- 1 tsp cumin powder
- 1 tsp coriander powder
- 3-6 cloves of garlic peeled and minced
- 1 inch piece of ginger peeled and grated
- 1 cup yogurt
- 2 tablespoon mint leaves (optional)
- 1 tsp salt

Method
1. Combine all the ingredients (except salmon) together with yogurt in a large resealable freezer bag. Mix well together.
2. Add salmon filets, toss until coated well. Marinate in the refrigerator overnight.
3. Set oven to broiler. Remove the salmon from the freezer bag and arrange it on a greased baking pan. Discard any excess marinade or use it to marinate another batch for the next day.
4. Broil for about 7-10 minutes (or about 4-6 minutes per side).

Serve with rice.

Recipe Notes:
1. Instead of mint, you can use cilantro, basil, or rosemary.
2. You could also bake the fish, in this case, bake it at 400 degrees Fahrenheit (205 C) for 10-12 minutes.

# My Recipe Notes

**Result:** Loved it     Okay ☑  Not for me ☒

**Spice Level:** Too Spicy 😄   Just Right 🙂   Not Spicy Enough 😎

**Date(s):**

**Comments:**

## TANDOORI SALMON

Most of you know about tandoori chicken, where spice marinated chicken is cooked in a clay oven. You can apply some of the same principles, using a conventional oven to bake, to make tandoori fish. Tandoori fish is very easy to make and is delicious.

Ingredients
- 2 lbs. salmon
- 2 tsp tandoori masala
- 1 cup yogurt
- ½ tsp salt

Method
1. Combine all the ingredients (except salmon) together with yogurt in a large resealable freezer bag. Mix well together.
2. Add salmon filets, toss until coated well. Marinate in the refrigerator overnight.
3. Set oven to broiler. Remove the salmon from the freezer bag and arrange it on a greased baking pan. Discard any excess marinade or use it to marinate another batch for the next day.
4. Broil for about 7-10 minutes (or about 4-6 minutes per side).

Serve as an appetizer or as a side dish.

## My Recipe Notes

**Result:** Loved it ♥   Okay ☑   Not for me ☒
**Spice Level:** Too Spicy 😊   Just Right ☺   Not Spicy Enough 😎
**Date(s):**
**Comments:**

## 15 Minute Spicy Fish Fry

This is a quick recipe that I use to make fish fry for my daughter who loves fried salmon. I use fresh or frozen salmon filets to make this. This recipe uses an air-fryer and is less messy and smelly than frying in oil. This is also healthier since little to no oil is used. Serve as a party appetizer or a snack item.

Ingredients

- 1 lb. salmon filet cut into 1-inch cubes
- ½ teaspoon turmeric powder
- ½-1 teaspoon chili powder
- ½ teaspoon black pepper
- 1-2 tsp ginger-garlic paste
- 1 tbsp breadcrumbs (optional)
- 1 tablespoon coconut or olive oil
- 1 tablespoon lime juice
- ½ teaspoon salt or to taste

Method
1. Mix fish cubes with all the ingredients in a large enough bowl and set aside for 15 minutes (or more)
2. Air fry for 10-15 minutes @ 400 degrees Fahrenheit (205 degrees C) or until done, tossing them over midway.

Recipe notes:
1. Instead of turmeric and chili powder separately, you could try with 1 teaspoon (or more) of other spice mixes such as tandoori chicken masala, curry masala, or garam masala. Each one will give you a different taste.
2. You can try the fish fry with and without ginger-garlic paste and see which one you like better. Most of the time I use ginger-garlic paste but it is good without as well.
3. If you like to have a crunch, sprinkle some breadcrumbs midway through frying.
4. If you like more acidity for the fish fry, dissolve 1-2 tsp tamarind paste in ½ cup water and add it in during step 1.
5. Marinating for a couple of hours or overnight gives better results.
6. Instead of air frying, you could bake the fish for 10-15 minutes at 400 degrees (205 degrees C).

# My Recipe Notes

**Result:** Loved it ♥   Okay ☑   Not for me ☒
**Spice Level:** Too Spicy 😄   Just Right 🙂   Not Spicy Enough 😎
**Date(s):**
**Comments:**

## Spicy Fish in Banana Leaf

There are many ways to cook fish with spices and herbs wrapped in a banana leaf. Banana leaves are used in many tropical locations for wrapping food while cooking or in some cases serving food (ex. the famous banana leaf meals in South India). Fresh banana leaves must be washed well in hot water and then tempered before using or it can break. For tempering gently steam the leaf or place it on a hot surface or fire for a few seconds until the leaf becomes pliable without breaking.

Beyond being a medium to wrap food for cooking or serving, banana leaves (and other leaves used similarly such as grape leaves, lotus leaves, etc.) contain important polyphenols that are natural antioxidants. Food cooked in or served on banana leaf absorbs some of the antioxidants and is therefore healthier.

If you do not have a banana tree in your yard, which most of us do not have, you can buy them at your local Asian store. They are very inexpensive and come in large flat packs wrapped in plastic. Below describes one such recipe with notes for different variations of this recipe.

Ingredients
- Salmon filet 4 pieces (2 in X 2 in)
- ½ tsp turmeric powder
- ½ tsp pepper powder (optional)
- ½ -1 tsp chili powder
- 1 tsp cumin powder
- ¼ - ½ cup freshly shredded coconut
- ½ tsp grated ginger
- 3-6 cloves of garlic peeled
- Juice from 1 lemon

Method
1. Marinate the fish with turmeric, salt, lemon juice, and half of the chili powder and set it aside for 20 minutes.
2. Grind coconut, ginger, garlic, cumin, black pepper, and the rest of the chili powder and make a paste.
3. Spread 4 banana leaves on a flat kitchen surface, lay the marinated fish, and apply the paste equally and evenly on all four filets.
4. Fold the banana leaves, seal them tight using kitchen twine and steam the fish in a steamer for about 10 minutes.

Recipe Notes:
1. Instead of spice powders, you could use whole spices – cumin seeds (1 tsp), whole dried chilies (3-4 nos.), black pepper (4-5 nos.). Either grind them as is along with coconut, ginger, and garlic in step 2 or roast them first and then grind. Roasting enhances the flavor of the spices).
2. You can include herbs of your choice – mint, cilantro, basil, or rosemary in step 3. Each of these herbs will provide a different taste and flavor. In addition to these herbs, you could also add curry leaves.
3. Instead of banana leaves, you can use bamboo leaves, lotus leaves, or grape leaves.

**Alternative Spicy Banana Leaf recipes**
1. Oven-baked spicy banana leaf salmon
    a. Follow the same steps 1-3 as in the earlier recipe.

b. Now seal the banana leaves and bake it in an oven for 10-15 minutes at 400 degrees Fahrenheit (205 degrees centigrade)

2. Grilled fish in banana leaf
   a. Same steps as the previous recipe except the fish now grilled on an open grill. In this case, make sure to have some extra layers of the banana leaf so when the outer layer becomes charred, the inner layers and fish is not burned.
   b. You could also wrap the banana leaf-wrapped fish in an outer layer of aluminum foil before grilling.

3. Spicy Green steamed/baked fish
   a. In the previous recipe, instead of spices, grind 2-3 green chilies, garlic, ginger, 1 cup mint or cilantro (or both), and use the green paste along with salt and lime juice.
   b. Wrap the fish in a banana leaf with the green sauce.
   c. Steam, bake, or grill the fish.
4. Salsa fish
   a. Follow step 1 in the recipe to marinate the fish. Now use mild, medium, or hot salsa or Picante sauce as per your liking to apply to the marinated fish before wrapping it in banana leaf. Steam, bake, or grill as detailed earlier.

Notes:

# My Recipe Notes

**Result:** Loved it ♥    Okay ☑    Not for me ☒

**Spice Level:** Too Spicy 😆    Just Right ☺    Not Spicy Enough 😎

**Date(s):**

**Comments:**

_____
_____
_____
_____
_____
_____
_____
_____
_____
_____
_____
_____
_____
_____
_____
_____
_____

## Spicy Grilled Fish

Ingredients
- 4 fish filets (about 1 lb.)
- 1 tsp chili flakes
- 1-2 tsp dark soy sauce
- 1-2 tsp red chili sauce
- 2 tsp ginger-garlic paste
- ½ tsp turmeric powder
- ½ tsp black pepper powder
- Juice of one lemon
- 2 tbsp olive oil
- ½ -1 tsp salt

Method
1. Sprinkle turmeric and pepper powder on both sides of the fish filet. Squeeze the lemon on both sides of the fish filet. Set aside.
2. Meanwhile mix chili flakes, soy sauce, red chili sauce, salt, and olive oil and make a marinade.
3. Apply marinade on both sides of the fish so that the marinade is well coated. Let it marinate for 20-30 minutes.
4. Heat a grill and apply 1-2 tsp oil on the pan.
5. Grill fish for about 2 minutes on both sides on medium. Baste the fish with any left-over marinade and grill for another minute on both sides.

Recipe Notes:
1. You can make variations of the same recipe by cooking the fish in different ways as below:
    a. Instead of grilling, bake the fish for about 10 minutes at 400 degrees Fahrenheit (or 205 degrees centigrade) in an oven. For baking, you could bake it on a pan or wrap the fish in a banana or some other leaf.
    b. Fry the fish in oil (olive oil, coconut, vegetable oil).
2. Instead of fish filet, you can use whole fish (cleaned with head or without head). If you use whole fish, make enough cuts on both sides of the fish so you can apply the marinade. If you are using a whole fish, increase the grilling time by another 10-15 minutes (5-7 minutes additional on both sides).

# My Recipe Notes

**Result:** Loved it ♥   Okay ☑   Not for me ☒
**Spice Level:** Too Spicy 😄   Just Right 🙂   Not Spicy Enough 😎
**Date(s):**
**Comments:**

Additional Notes:

## CHAPTER 2. SPICY CURRIED FISH

Spice blends were used in cooking during the days of Indus Valley Civilization, almost 4000 years ago as many spices were cultivated in the Indian subcontinent. The locals mixed and matched these spices in the preparation of food. Mostly, these spices were used to enhance food flavor or to increase the shelf life of the prepared food as no modern food preservation was available. Over time, these ancient civilizations recognized that these spice blends have health benefits beyond flavoring or preserving food.

While the use of spice blends dates 4000 years ago, the idea of "curry" powder came from the 18th-century English colonists who were part of the South Asian spice trade. English colonists did not quite understand the local population's preparation and use of spice blends. They called anything prepared using a spice blend, "curry".

The word "curry" originated from the word "*Kari*" which means "sauce or relish for rice" in Tamil, a language spoken in the southern part of India, Sri Lanka, and parts of southeast Asia.

Today, curry or curry soup is a popular dish all over the world and especially in the south and south east Asia. Fish is abundant in many parts of this region due to proximity to Indian ocean and Arabian sea as well as many freshwater lakes and rivers. Fish curry is made using locally available ingredients such as spices, coconut, and tamarind, among others.

### 10 MINUTE SALMON CURRY

**Ingredients**
- 1lbs. skinless salmon cut into 2-inch pieces
- 1 tsp chili powder
- 1 tsp coriander powder
- Black pepper powder - ¼ tsp
- 1 medium onion
- Grated ginger 2 tsp
- Crushed garlic 4-5 cloves
- Curry leaves - 2 sprigs (optional)
- 1 cup medium salsa or Picante sauce

Method
1. Combine all the spices powders – chili, turmeric, coriander, and pepper powder in a bowl. Add 2 tsp or just enough water to make a thick paste and set aside.
2. Heat oil in a pan. Add ginger, garlic, onions, optional green chilies, and curry leaves. Sauté until onion becomes translucent.
3. Add the spice paste and mix well on low flame (Wet the masala to make sure it gets fried but not burnt).

4. After a few minutes (once masala gets fried), add salsa and mix. Now add salmon pieces. Gently mix so the salmon pieces are covered in the sauce, but the salmon is not broken. Cover and cook for 5-10 minutes.

This is a quick way to make salmon. The salsa or Picante sauce gives the acidity, the spices give the heat, and it is super easy. Goes with rice or bread.

Recipe Notes:
1. This recipe may also be used to make fish curry from canned tuna, sardine, or any other canned fish. Follow the same recipe and you will get yummy fish curry out of bland canned fish in no time.
2. Chopped Jalapenos may be added for additional heat.
3. Instead of individual spices, you can use 1-2 tsp of curry powder, or garam masala.

# My Recipe Notes

**Result:** Loved it ♥    Okay ☑    Not for me ☒
**Spice Level:** Too Spicy 😆    Just Right 🙂    Not Spicy Enough 😎
**Date(s):**
**Comments:**

## SALMON WITH GREEN MANGO

**Ingredients**
- 2 lbs. skinless salmon cut into 2-inch pieces
- Chili powder 1-4 tsp (depending on your tolerance level)
- Turmeric 1 tsp
- Coriander powder - 1 tbsp
- Fenugreek powder - 1/4 tsp, or fenugreek seeds ½ tsp
- Black pepper powder - ¼ tsp
- Mustard seeds - 1/2 tsp
- 1 medium onion
- Grated ginger 2 tsp
- Crushed garlic 4-5 cloves
- Curry leaves - 2 sprigs (optional)
- Washed and cut green mango (with skin or skin removed depending on your preference) – 2 cups
- Water-1 to 1.5 cups (or as required)
- Salt to taste
- 2-4 sliced green chilies or jalapeños, seeds removed (optional)

Method
1. Combine all the spices powders – chili, turmeric, coriander, fenugreek, and pepper powder in a bowl. Add 2 tsp or just enough water to make a thick paste and set aside.
2. Heat oil in a pan and splutter mustard seeds and fenugreek (if using seeds instead of powder).
3. Add ginger, garlic, onions, optional green chilies, and curry leaves. Sauté until onion becomes translucent.
4. Add the masala paste and mix well on low flame (Wet the masala with oil to make sure it gets fried but not burnt).
5. After a few minutes (once the masala gets fried), add about 2 cups of water. Mix gently and then add the cut mango pieces.
6. Cover it and bring it to a boil on medium heat. Now add individual fish pieces into the pan.
7. Mix gently, making sure the fish pieces are not broken up and that all the pieces are coated with the gravy.
8. Cover the pan and cook it for about 20 minutes or until the fish is done and the gravy is thick. Switch off the flame and keep it covered for 30 minutes for the fish to soak in the spices and mango flavor.

Serve with rice or bread.

Notes:
1. Paprika may be used instead of chili powder if you desire to make it less spicy.
2. Any other fish may be used instead of salmon.
3. Instead of mango, tamarind, or Garcinia Cambogia available in Asian stores may be used.
4. Green chilies or jalapeños add more heat to the fish curry. Use depending on your taste.

# My Recipe Notes

**Result:** Loved it ♥   Okay ☑   Not for me ☒

**Spice Level:** Too Spicy 😅   Just Right 🙂   Not Spicy Enough 😎

**Date(s):**

**Comments:**

## SPICY PICKLED FISH

Indian and South Asian pickles are very spicy unlike the pickles in North America and Europe. The Asian pickle spice mix generally includes a generous amount of chili powder, turmeric, mustard seeds, fenugreek seeds, and asafetida. While spicy vegetable pickles are very popular, meat, fish, and shrimp can also be pickled. There are many ways to pickle fish. The idea is to soak marinated and fried fish pieces in a sauce containing a lot of chili and other ingredients and vinegar. Pickle can last several weeks in the fridge and is consumed in moderation as they are really spicy.

Ingredients
- 2 lbs. fish filet cut into 1-inch pieces
- 4 tablespoon vegetable oil
- 1 cup finely chopped onions
- 2-4 tablespoon red chili powder
- 1 teaspoon turmeric powder
- 2-inch ginger piece finely chopped (or paste)
- 10-12 cloves of garlic chopped (or paste)
- 10 green chilies or jalapeno peppers chopped (optional)
- 2 spring curry leaves
- 1 teaspoon mustard seeds
- 1 teaspoon fenugreek seeds
- ½-1 cup vinegar (white/ red wine / rice wine/apple cider)
- ½ teaspoon salt or to taste
- 4-6 tablespoon oil

Method
1. Use 1 tablespoon chili powder, ½ teaspoon turmeric, 1 tablespoon vinegar, and salt to mix with the fish. Marinate for 30 minutes – 1 hr. or overnight,
2. Heat 2-3 tablespoon oil and fry the marinated fish pieces on both sides for about 4-6 minutes or until the fish is fried. Remove the fish and set aside.
3. Add the rest of the oil in the same pan, crackle mustard seeds, and fenugreek seeds. sauté onions, garlic, ginger, green chilies, and curry leaves for 1-2 minutes. Add rest of the spices and mix for another 1-2 minutes or the spices are cooked.
4. Now add the fried fish pieces. Mix well.
5. Add vinegar, cover, and simmer for 1-2 minutes.
6. Add additional salt if required and mix. Let it cool down.
7. Transfer it into a glass jar and use it as a condiment to add flavor to your dishes or use as a side dish. It should last in the fridge for at least a month.

Recipe notes:
1. Though vegetable oil is used in the recipe as it is easier to buy, mustard oil is the best oil to make spicy pickles.
2. There are several alternative ways to make this pickle and each may come out a bit different than the recipe given above.
3. Instead of frying the fish in oil, you could bake it or air-fry it before mixing with the pickle masala.
4. The same recipe may be tried without marinating if you are short on time.

5. You could substitute 2-3 tablespoons of lemon juice instead of vinegar.
6. Try the same recipe with different vinegar (apple cider, white vinegar, wine vinegar, etc.) and see how you like it.
7. Since this dish can be kept for a long time in the fridge and is only used as a side in moderation, care must be taken every time you use a spoon to take pickle from the jar. The spoon needs to be dry and clean or the pickle could go bad.
8. Usually, white firm fish such as tuna, marlin, etc. is better to use as they will stay firm and don't break while mixing with pickle sauce. However, any kind of fish can be pickled including salmon, tilapia, bass, etc. Make sure to remove bones before frying.

Notes:

# My Recipe Notes

**Result:** Loved it ♥   Okay ☑   Not for me ☒

**Spice Level:** Too Spicy 😅   Just Right 🙂   Not Spicy Enough 😎

**Date(s):**

**Comments:**

## Recipes Using Canned Fish

If you have read my other books, I am a stickler for healthy, fresh, and natural ingredients. At the same time, I am also a fan of quick and easy recipes.

Canned fish provides a convenient, easy, and quick alternative to using fresh fish. As I write this book, the COVID-19 pandemic of 2020 is raging, and people are going out less frequently to shop. Canned fish can be stored for a long time and is a very good alternative to fresh fish for which you need to shop more frequently. Moreover, they are inexpensive and save a lot of time while cooking. Using canned fish is also a good choice, especially if you are a student, on a budget, or simply pressed for time.

## Quick Canned Sardine Masala

Basic Ingredients
- 2-3 cans of sardine
- 2 tsp coconut or olive oil
- ½ pepper powder
- 1-2 tsp curry powder/garam masala
- 1 cup salsa, Picante sauce, or tomato puree
- ½ cup vegetable broth/water

Method
1. Heat oil in a medium non-stick pan, add the spices, and cook them on low heat for 20-30 seconds. Make sure the spices do not burn.
2. Add salsa/Picante sauce/tomato puree.
3. Add canned sardines. Add ½ cup water or vegetable broth. Cover and simmer for 2-3 minutes and quick and spicy sardine masala is ready.

Recipe Notes:
1. You can do a little more elaborate preparation of the same recipe by sautéing one chopped-up onion, 1 tsp grated ginger, and garlic in step 1 before adding spices.
2. If you like it spicier, add 1 tsp chili powder in step 1. You can also add chopped up green chilies.
3. Salsa, Picante sauce, and tomato puree give the required acidity. Each of these also has a somewhat different taste.
4. You can add cilantro to garnish.

## My Recipe Notes

**Result:** Loved it ♥   Okay ☑   Not for me ☒
**Spice Level:** Too Spicy 😊   Just Right ☺   Not Spicy Enough 😎
**Date(s):**
**Comments:**

## QUICK FISH CURRY WITH CANNED TUNA

Basic Ingredients
- 3-4 canned chunk light tuna
- 2 tsp coconut or olive oil
- 1 medium onion sliced
- 1 tsp turmeric powder
- ½ pepper powder
- 1-2 medium tomatoes chopped
- ½ tsp salt (or to taste)
- ¼ cup fresh cilantro chopped
- ½ cup vegetable broth

Optional Ingredients
- 1-2 jalapenos sliced (seeds out/in)
- 2-3 cloves of garlic crushed
- ½ inch ginger root chopped into fine pieces or paste
- ¼ cup grated coconut

Method
1. Heat oil in a medium non-stick pan, add onions, and optional garlic, ginger, and jalapenos. Stir until the onion becomes translucent.
2. Add turmeric and pepper stir for 2 minutes.
3. Add chopped tomatoes, mix well, and cook for 3-4 minutes.
4. Add tuna. Cover and simmer for 10-15 minutes, or until the tomatoes are cooked.
5. Switch off heat. Add the cilantro and coconut.

Mix well and serve hot with rice or bread.

Note 1: There are many optional ingredients listed, one could use all of them or pick and choose based on your taste.

# My Recipe Notes

**Result:** Loved it ♥   Okay ☑   Not for me ☒

**Spice Level:** Too Spicy 😊   Just Right ☺   Not Spicy Enough 😎

**Date(s):**

**Comments:**

## GOAN FISH CURRY

Goa is a coastal state south of Mumbai in India stretching along the coastlines of the Arabian sea. Goa was a Portuguese colony until it was integrated into Indian Union in 1961. Goa is a beautiful place with several 17th-century churches, sandy beaches, tropical plantations, and fishing villages. There are many variations of the Goan fish curry recipe. The main thing to remember is that this recipe usually uses freshly grated coconut for creaminess and tamarind paste to give the tanginess. Some recipes roast the spices first before grinding while others grind the whole spices first before sautéing.

Ingredients
- 2 lbs. fish of your choice, cleaned, washed, and cut into pieces
- 1-2 tsp chili powder or whole red chilies 4-8
- 1 tsp turmeric 1 tsp
- 2 tbsp coconut oil
- 2 tsp coriander seeds
- 1 tsp cumin seeds
- ½ tsp mustard seeds
- 5-10 black peppercorns
- 2 tsp grated ginger
- 4-5 cloves crushed garlic
- ½ -1 cup coconut – freshly grated preferred, if not use flakes
- 2 tsp tamarind paste/pulp
- 1 tsp garam masala (optional)
- 1 to 1.5 cups of water (or as required)
- Salt to taste
- 2-4 sliced green chilies or jalapeños, seeds removed (optional)

Method
1. Marinate the fish with turmeric, salt, and half of the chili powder and set it aside for 20 minutes.
2. Roast the whole spices (coriander, cumin, peppercorns, red chilies), then set aside.
3. Sauté onions, ginger, garlic in 1 tbsp oil
4. Grind the roasted spices and sautéed onion, garlic, ginger, and coconut and make a paste.
5. Heat oil in a deep bottom pan and sauté the ground paste from the step for about 2-3 minutes.
6. Once the spices are cooked, add water and tamarind paste and bring to a boil. Make sure tamarind paste is fully dissolved.
7. Add fish pieces. Make sure the pieces are fully covered in the sauce. Cook for about 10 minutes or until the fish is fully cooked.
8. Add salt to taste.
9. Let it sit for 30 minutes to cool down and for the fish to fully absorb the spices and the tanginess of the tamarind.

Serve with rice.

There are many variations to Goan fish curry. See the notes below to try different variations and make your own special recipe.

Notes:

1. Roasting the whole spices increases the aroma and flavor of the curry. If you would like to skip this step, simply add the spices into the grinder along with grated coconut and other ingredients.
2. You can use any kind of fish for this recipe.
3. Instead of tamarind or in addition to tamarind, you may also add kokum or the black tamarind.
4. You can also add tomatoes if you like in this recipe.
5. Instead of whole spices, you may use spice powders – 1-2 tsp coriander powder, 1 tsp cumin powder, 1-2 tsp chili powder, and ½ -1 tsp turmeric. Mix the spices with water and make a paste. Grind coconut, ginger, and garlic separately and use both pastes in step 5.

Notes:

## My Recipe Notes

**Result:** Loved it ♥   Okay ☑   Not for me ☒

**Spice Level:** Too Spicy 😆   Just Right 🙂   Not Spicy Enough 😎

**Date(s):**

**Comments:**

## Fish Makhani

Fish Makhani is a North Indian recipe that has fish cooked in a creamy and buttery gravy. Typical preparation of fish makhani involves lightly frying the fish in oil and then cooking in a thick sauce made of spices, herbs, tomato puree, and yogurt. This dish may be served with rice or Indian bread. Any firm white fish may be used.

Basic Ingredients
- 2 lb. fish filet cut into pieces
- 1 ½ cup tomato puree
- 1 cup low far yogurt
- 1 stick butter
- 2 tbsp vegetable oil
- 1 tsp turmeric powder
- ½ pepper powder
- 1-2 tsp chili powder
- 1 tsp cumin powder
- 1-2 tsp garam masala/curry powder (optional)
- ½ tsp salt (or to taste)
- 1-2 tsp ginger garlic paste
- ½ cup vegetable broth

Method
1. Marinate the fish with turmeric, salt, and half of the chili powder and set it aside for 20 minutes.
2. Heat oil in a medium non-stick pan and shallow fry the fish for about 2-3 minutes until golden brown on both sides and set the fried fish aside.
3. In the same pan, melt butter, sauté ginger and garlic paste, add cumin powder, rest of chili powder, black pepper powder, and optional garam masala/curry powder. Mix on low heat until fragrant (about 1-2 min). Now add tomato puree and mix well. Add ½ cup vegetable broth or water. Let it simmer for a minute. Add yogurt and mix.
4. Now add the fried fish. Let the fish be coated well with the sauce. Simmer it for a few minutes.
5. Switch off heat, garnish with cilantro and serve.

Mix well and serve hot as a side dish with rice or bread.

Recipe Notes:
1. There are many optional ingredients listed, one could use all of them or pick and choose based on your taste.

# My Recipe Notes

**Result:** Loved it ♥  Okay ☑  Not for me ☒
**Spice Level:** Too Spicy 😊  Just Right 🙂  Not Spicy Enough 😎
**Date(s):**
**Comments:**

## Fish in Yogurt Sauce

Fish cooked in yogurt sauce is a dish that has origins in Bengali cuisine. This is a simple recipe where the fish is marinated with turmeric and salt and then cooked in a sauce of yogurt and spices.

Ingredients
- 2 lbs. fish cut into pieces
- 2 tsp turmeric powder
- ½ tsp pepper powder (optional)
- ½ -1 tsp chili powder (optional)
- 1 tsp cumin seeds
- 1 medium red onion chopped
- 3-6 cloves of garlic peeled
- ½ cup yogurt
- 2-3 green chilies/jalapenos slit (optional)
- 2 tablespoons of oil
- ½ tsp mustard seeds

Method
1. Marinate the fish with turmeric and salt. Set it aside for 20 minutes.
2. Grind onions, garlic, cumin, black pepper, and chili powder and make a paste.
3. Heat oil in a pan, crackle mustard seeds. Add the paste from step 2, green chilies, sauté for 1-2 minutes.
4. Add 1 cup water, bring to a boil. Now add the marinated fish. Gently swirl the pan so the fish is coated with the sauce. Bring to a boil.
5. Now add yogurt. Mix well, gently, making sure the fish pieces are not broken.
6. Cover and simmer for 2-3 minutes or until fish is fully cooked and covered well with the sauce.

Serve with rice.

## My Recipe Notes

**Result:** Loved it ♥   Okay ☑   Not for me ☒

**Spice Level:** Too Spicy 😅   Just Right 🙂   Not Spicy Enough 😎

**Date(s):**

**Comments:**

## Chettinadu Fish Curry

Chettinadu is a region in the south Indian state of Tamil Nadu that is known for its distinct cuisine ([https://en.wikipedia.org/wiki/Chettinad_cuisine](https://en.wikipedia.org/wiki/Chettinad_cuisine)). While Chettinadu cuisine is predominantly vegetarian based, Chettinadu chicken and Chettinadu fish curry are very popular. Chettinadu cuisine uses freshly ground spices, coconut, yogurt, and tamarind, among others.

**Ingredients**
- 2 lbs. of mackerel/sardine/pomfret - cleaned
- coconut oil – 2 tbsp

For the masala paste
- 1 medium onion chopped
- 2 medium tomatoes
- 2-4 tsp chili powder
- ½ tsp turmeric powder
- 1 tsp coriander seeds
- 1 tsp fennel seeds
- 1 tsp peppercorns
- 1 tsp cumin seeds
- 1 inch piece of ginger grated
- 1 cup grated coconut
- 5-6 garlic cloves crushed
- 1 lemon size tamarind
- 1-2 cups of water

For frying
- ½ tsp mustard seeds
- ½ tsp Fenugreek seeds
- 2-4 whole red chilies
- 2 spring curry leaves
- 1 onion chopped
- 1-2 green chilies (optional)
- Salt to taste

Method
1. Roast spices for the paste and coconut in a pan over medium heat. Transfer that to a grinder. Now add oil in the same pan, sauté onions, tamarind, ginger, garlic, and tomatoes.
2. In a blender or grinder, grind all the ingredients from step 1. Add a couple of tablespoons of water, if needed, to make it a thick, smooth paste.
3. Heat oil in a deep bottom pan, add oil, crackle mustard seeds. While mustard seeds are crackling, add fenugreek seeds, curry leaves, and red chilies. Add onions, and green chilies. Sauté for about a minute or until onion becomes translucent.
4. Add the curry paste from the blender/grinder. Mix well, then add one or two cups of water (depending on how much sauce you want for the curry) and mix again. You may use the water to wash the sides of the blender to get as much curry paste from the blender (instead of wasting the paste stuck to the sides). Cover and bring to a boil.

5. Add cut and washed fish pieces. Gently swirl the pot or use a spoon to mix gently so the fish is fully covered with the sauce. Cook covered for about 5-10 minutes or until the fish is cooked well.

Serve with rice.

Recipe Notes:
1. Instead of whole spices, you may use powders – 1 tsp coriander powder, 1 tsp cumin powder, ½- 1 tsp black pepper powder, and 1 tsp turmeric powder.
2. If your spice tolerance level is low or you are starting out using spice, you may want to reduce the quantities of the spices.
3. If you are a coconut lover, you could increase the amount of coconut used. Freshly grated coconut is always better, but you can also use store-bought coconut flakes (unsweetened).
4. As an alternative recipe, you could sauté half of the onions, ginger, and garlic with tomatoes and then grind it along with fresh coconut to create the paste. In this method, the powdered spices are then sautéed with the other half of onions, garlic, ginger, green chilies before adding the spice paste and water.
5. Tamarind may be soaked in water and tamarind water can be used instead of the whole tamarind.
6. You can use ¼ cup chopped cilantro to garnish.

Notes:

# My Recipe Notes

**Result:** Loved it ♥   Okay ☑   Not for me ☒
**Spice Level:** Too Spicy 😅   Just Right 🙂   Not Spicy Enough 😎
**Date(s):**
**Comments:**

## Malabar Fish Curry

Malabar refers to a coastal region on the southwest coast of India. This coast region covers a narrow coastal plain of present-day Kerala and Karnataka states of India. This region is essential sandwiched between the Western Ghats mountain range and the Arabian sea. As the Western Ghats traps the monsoon rains, this region is beautiful and known for its greenery. This coastal area is rich in fish, filled with coconut palm trees, and famous for its spices. So, it is not a surprise that the entire region's cuisine was influenced by the geography and the availability of spices, as well as the abundance of coconuts.

As this region is quite vast, about 1000 miles long, there are several regional variations to a typical Malabar recipe such as Mangalorean fish curry, Goan fish curry, and Kerala fish curry. Some of them are described in the recipe notes.

**Ingredients**

- 2 lbs. salmon (or your choice fish) cut into pieces
- coconut oil – 2 tbsp
- ½ tsp mustard seeds
- ½ tsp Fenugreek seeds
- 1 medium onion chopped
- 2-3 medium tomatoes
- 1 tsp ginger paste
- 1 tsp garlic paste
- 1-2 cups of water
- 2-4 whole red chilies
- 1 tsp turmeric powder
- 1 tsp coriander seeds
- 1 tsp cumin seeds
- 1 cup grated coconut
- 1-2 green chilies (optional)
- Salt to taste

Method

1. In a food processor, blender, or grinder, grind the coconut, coriander, cumin, chilies, and turmeric into a thick curry paste. Add a couple of teaspoons of water if the paste is too dry.
2. Heat oil in a deep bottom pan, add oil, crackle mustard seeds. While mustard seeds are crackling, add fenugreek seeds. Add onions, green chilies, ginger, and garlic paste. Sauté for about a minute or until onion becomes translucent. Add tomatoes. Mix well and cook for a couple of minutes covered, stirring occasionally.
3. Add curry paste from the blender/grinder. Mix well. Add one or two cups of water (depending on how much sauce you want for the curry) and mix well. You may use the water to wash the sides of the blender to get as much curry paste from the blender (instead of wasting the paste stuck to the sides). Cover and bring to a boil.
4. Add cut and washed fish pieces. Gently swirl the pot or use a spoon to mix gently (so the fish does not break) so the fish is fully covered with the sauce. Cook covered for about 5-10 minutes or until the fish is cooked well.

Serve with rice.
Recipe Notes:

1. Instead of whole spices, you may use powders – ½ -1 tsp chili powder, 1 tsp coriander powder, 1 tsp cumin powder, and 1 tsp turmeric powder.
2. Instead of or in addition to tomatoes, you could add tamarind paste, black tamarind, or lemon juice to give acidity.

Notes:

# My Recipe Notes

**Result:** Loved it ♥   Okay ☑   Not for me ☒

**Spice Level:** Too Spicy 😆   Just Right 🙂   Not Spicy Enough 😎

**Date(s):**

**Comments:**

## Coconut Milk Fish Curry

This is a variation of Malabar fish curry. In this recipe, instead of using a grinder to grind grated coconut and spices to a paste, coconut milk is used – either canned or squeezing juice out of freshly grated coconut.

**Ingredients**
- 2 lbs. fish cut into pieces
- coconut oil – 2 tbsp
- ½ tsp mustard seeds
- ½ tsp Fenugreek seeds
- 1 medium onion chopped
- 2-3 medium tomatoes
- 1 tsp grated ginger
- 1 can coconut milk

- 1 tsp chili powder
- 1 tsp turmeric powder
- 1 tsp coriander powder
- 1-2 green chilies (optional)
- 2 sprigs curry leaves (optional)
- Salt to taste

Method
1. Heat oil in a deep bottom pan, add oil, crackle mustard seeds. While mustard seeds are crackling, add fenugreek seeds. Add onions, green chilies, ginger, and garlic. Sauté for about a minute or until onion becomes translucent.
2. Add spice powders and tomatoes. Mix well and cook for a couple of minutes covered, stirring occasionally.
3. Add coconut milk. Cover and bring to a boil.
4. Add cut and washed fish pieces. Gently swirl the pot or use a spoon to mix gently so the fish is fully covered with the sauce. Cook covered for about 5-10 minutes or until the fish is cooked well.

Serve with rice.

# My Recipe Notes

**Result:** Loved it ♥　　Okay ☑　　Not for me ☒

**Spice Level:** Too Spicy 😄　Just Right ☺　Not Spicy Enough 😎

**Date(s):**

**Comments:**

## Kerala Fish Curry

Kerala is along the Malabar coast and this recipe is a variation of Malabar fish curry. This recipe uses a local ingredient Garcinia Cambogia or Malabar tamarind (also known as *kudam puli* in the local language) as it is abundantly available in Kerala and it gives the acidity or sourness taste that goes with fish curry.

**Ingredients**

- 2 lbs. fish cut into pieces
- 2 tbsp coconut oil –
- ½ tsp mustard seeds
- ½ tsp Fenugreek seeds
- 1 medium onion chopped
- 1 tsp ginger grated ginger
- 2-3 tsp chili powder
- ½ tsp turmeric powder
- 1 tsp coriander powder
- 2 springs curry leaves (optional)
- 1-2 green chilies slit (optional)
- 3-4 pieces of black tamarind or garcinia cambogia (washed and soaked in water)
- Salt to taste

Method

1. Combine all the spices powders – chili, turmeric, coriander -- together in a bowl. Add 2 tsp or just enough water to make a thick paste and set aside.
2. Heat oil in a pan and splutter mustard seeds and fenugreek (if seeds used instead of powder).
3. Add ginger, garlic, onions, optional green chilies, and curry leaves. Sauté until onion becomes translucent.
4. Add the masala paste and mix well on low flame (Making the powders into a paste helps to get it fried but not burnt).
5. After few minutes (once the masala gets fried), add about 2 cups of water mix and then add the soaked in Malabar tamarind along with the water.
6. Cover and bring it to a boil on medium heat. Now add individual fish pieces into the pan.
7. Mix gently, making sure the fish pieces are not broken up and that all the pieces are coated with the gravy.
8. Cover the pan and cook it for about 15 minutes or until the fish is done and the gravy is thick. Switch off the flame and keep it covered for 30 minutes for the fish to soak in the spices and absorbs the spices and sourness.

Serve with rice or bread.

# My Recipe Notes

**Result:** Loved it ♥   Okay ☑   Not for me ☒

**Spice Level:** Too Spicy 😊   Just Right ☺   Not Spicy Enough 😎

**Date(s):**

**Comments:**

## Mangalore Fish Curry

Mangalore is region along the Malabar coast. This is another variation of Malabar fish curry. In this recipe, whole spices are roasted first and then ground along with coconut, ginger, garlic, onions, tamarind, and then fish is cooked in the rich, thick sauce.

**Ingredients**
- 2 lbs. fish cut into pieces (any kind of fish)
- 2 tbsp coconut oil (any kind)
- ½ tsp mustard seeds
- ½ tsp Fenugreek seeds
- 1 medium onion chopped
- One lime size ball of tamarind
- 1 tsp ginger grated ginger
- 5-6 cloves of garlic peeled
- ½ cup freshly grated coconut
- 5-10 whole red chilies
- 5-10 whole Kashmiri chilies (optional)
- 1 tsp coriander seeds
- 1 tsp cumin seeds
- 1 tsp turmeric powder
- 1-2 green chilies (optional)
- 2 springs curry leaves (optional)
- Salt to taste

Method
1. First gently roast the whole spices – chilies, cumin, coriander, mustard, and fenugreek until the spices are aromatic. A couple of minutes should do. Do not burn the spices.
2. Now grind the roasted spices along with coconut, garlic, ginger, onions, tamarind, and optional green chilies and make a smooth paste.
3. Now heat oil in a pan and transfer the smooth paste into the pan. Careful not to splatter. Sauté the masala paste for about a minute.
4. Now use 1-2 cups of water and wash the leftover paste from the grinder into the pan. Mix well and add more if needed to make the sauce your desired or preferred consistency level. Cover and bring it to a boil.
5. Add cut and washed fish pieces. Use a spoon to gently mix so the fish is fully covered with the sauce. Cook covered for about 5-10 minutes or until the fish is cooked well.

Serve with rice.

Recipe Notes:
1. Instead of whole spices, you may use powders – ½ -1 tsp chili powder, 1 tsp coriander powder, 1 tsp cumin powder, and 1 tsp turmeric powder.
2. Instead of or in addition to tomatoes, you could add tamarind paste, black tamarind, or lemon juice to give the sour taste or acidity.

# My Recipe Notes

**Result:** Loved it ♥   Okay ☑   Not for me ☒
**Spice Level:** Too Spicy 😊   Just Right 🙂   Not Spicy Enough 😎
**Date(s):**
**Comments:**

_____
_____
_____
_____
_____
_____
_____
_____
_____
_____
_____
_____
_____
_____
_____
_____
_____
_____
_____
_____

## TURMERIC FISH

This is a very quick and healthy recipe. Turmeric is a medicinal and healing spice with many health benefits.

Ingredients
- 2-3 pieces of tilapia filets
- 2 tbsp olive oil
- 1 tbsp butter
- 2 tsp turmeric powder
- 1 tsp cumin powder
- ½ - 1 tsp chili powder
- 2 tsp lemon juice
- ½ tsp black pepper powder
- ½ tsp salt (or to taste)

Method
1. Combine oil, spice powders and lemon juice, salt, and pepper.
2. Coat the tilapia filets on both sides with spice sauce. Set aside for 10-15 minutes.
3. In a pan, melt butter and cook the fish for 1-2 minutes on each side on high heat.
4. Serve with rice.

Recipe Notes
1. You could make a turmeric curry out of this recipe by making a turmeric base sauce and cooking fish in the sauce.
    a. Cut fish into 2-inch pieces.
    b. Chop a full onion.
    c. Sauté onion in oil. Add 2 tsp ginger garlic paste. Add turmeric and other spices.
    d. Add 2 cups of water and 2 tbsp lemon juice and bring to a boil.
    e. Now add fish and cook covered for 15-20 minutes.

# My Recipe Notes

**Result:** Loved it ♥   Okay ☑   Not for me ☒

**Spice Level:** Too Spicy 😄   Just Right 🙂   Not Spicy Enough 😎

**Date(s):**

**Comments:**

# Chapter 3. International Spicy Fish Recipes

## Seafood Paella

Paella is a rice dish that originated in the Spanish city of Valencia, on the east coast of Spain, and is considered one of the best-known dishes of Spanish Cuisine. Paella is usually cooked in a shallow "frying pan" where the name comes from. Paella may be made with meat, vegetable, or seafood. Seafood paella is cooked more frequently and more popular due to the easy availability of seafood in the Valencia region. The recipe below is not traditional paella but an adapted version with the use of spices and herbs.

Basic Ingredients
- 3-4 cups of basmati rice (or rice of your choice)
- 4 tbsp olive oil
- 1 medium red onion sliced
- 1-2 medium tomatoes chopped
- ½ tsp salt (or to taste)
- ¼ cup fresh cilantro chopped
- 3 cups of fish or chicken broth
- 10-12 mussels, cleaned
- 12-16 shrimp with shell on (remove shells, if you prefer)
- A pinch of saffron
- 2-3 small squid, cleaned and cut into ¼ inch wide rings
- 1-2 jalapenos sliced (optional, seeds out/in)
- 2-3 cloves of garlic chopped
- ½ inch ginger root chopped into fine pieces or paste
- 1 tsp chili flakes
- ½ - 1 tsp curry powder/garam masala (optional)
- 1 cup white wine (optional)

Method
1. Wash and soak the rice in water.
2. Heat oil in a thick bottom pan, add onions, garlic, ginger, and optional jalapenos. Stir until the onion becomes translucent.
3. Add chili flakes and optional curry powder. Sauté for about one minute or until the spices are cooked. Add chopped tomatoes, mussels, squid, and shrimp. Mix all the ingredients. Add soaked rice and mix.
4. Add fish/chicken stock. Cover and cook on medium heat until rice is cooked.
5. Garnish with cilantro and serve.

# My Recipe Notes

**Result:** Loved it ♥  Okay ☑  Not for me ☒

**Spice Level:** Too Spicy 😅  Just Right ☺  Not Spicy Enough 😎

**Date(s):**

**Comments:**

## SPICY KOREAN FISH STEW

Korean fish stew is a heart-warming and spice Korean dish that is made with whole fish pieces, including fish head, and vegetables such as Korean radish, onions, and others. This recipe is not an authentic Korean fish stew recipe but a simpler, spicier, and quicker version of the popular preparation.

Ingredients

- 2 lbs. Whole fish cleaned including fish head cut into medium size (2in) pieces
- 6 cups of water
- 1 medium onion sliced
- 1lbs. Korean radish sliced
- 1 tsp turmeric powder
- ½ tsp black pepper powder
- 10-12 garlic cloves crushed
- 1-2 jalapeno pepper sliced diagonally
- 3-4 spring of green onions sliced diagonally
- 1-2 tsp grated ginger
- 1-2 tbsp Korean hot pepper paste
- 1 tbsp soy sauce
- 1 tbsp fish sauce
- 2-3 tbsp cooking wine/rice wine
- Salt to taste

Method

1. Mix the spices, garlic, ginger, soy sauce, fish sauce, wine, and salt in the water to make a broth to cook the fish and vegetables in.
2. Layer the vegetables – radish, onions, and fish in a cooking pot and pour enough broth to cover the fish with the broth.
3. Covered cook until fish is cooked, and sauce is thickened. Add jalapenos and green onions mid-way through cooking or about 10 minutes in.

Serve with rice.

Recipe Notes:

1. You can garnish with sesame seeds or herbs of your choice – chopped up cilantro, mint, or basil.
2. If Korean radish is not available, you can use red radishes to replace it.
3. Though not used in authentic recipes, you can try adding cut celery stalks and/or bell peppers. You can also add dried kelp (first boil it before adding).
4. You may also try adding squash, tofu, or mushrooms. Mix and match these additional ingredients to your liking.

## My Recipe Notes

**Result:** Loved it ♥   Okay ☑   Not for me ☒

**Spice Level:** Too Spicy 😅   Just Right 🙂   Not Spicy Enough 😎

**Date(s):**

**Comments:**

## SPICY MEDITERRANEAN SHAKSHUKA FISH #1

Shakshuka is usually an egg dish, usually eaten for breakfast in the Middle East, Israel, and parts of Africa. Shakshuka ingredients usually include tomatoes, onions, garlic, spices, and eggs. This recipe is adapted for fish preparation.

Ingredients
- 2 lbs. fish filet cut into 2-inch-wide pieces (Tilapia, Catfish, or your choice of fish)
- 1 medium onion, diced
- 3-5 garlic cloves, chopped
- 3 medium tomatoes cut into chunks
- 2 tablespoon extra-virgin olive oil
- ¼ cup cilantro and ¼ cup parsley, chopped
- Salt to taste
- ½ cup pitted, chopped olives
- ½ cup red bell pepper diced into 1-inch chunks
- ½-1 tsp chili powder
- ½ tsp turmeric powder
- 1 tsp cumin powder
- 2-3 tsp paprika
- ½ tsp black pepper powder
- 1-2 tsp lemon juice

Method
1. First marinate fish with salt, ½ tsp chili powder, and ½ tsp turmeric powder, and lemon juice.
2. Heat oil in a non-stick large enough saucepan over medium heat.
3. Add onions and garlic. Sauté until onions become translucent.
4. Add spices.
5. Add tomatoes and bell pepper. Mix well. Cover and cook on low flame for 5-10 minutes or until tomatoes are sufficiently wilted. If needed, stir occasionally so it does not stick to the pan. You can add olives either now or after the fish is cooked.
6. Make a well or space within the sauce using a spatula and lay the fish pieces directly into this space. Repeat this process until all pieces are added. Pour sauce over the fish so it is fully immersed.
7. Cover and simmer for 10-15 minutes or until fish is cooked.
8. Sprinkle black pepper powder, cilantro/parsley, or other herbs (mint, tarragon, chives, or green onions) and serve.

Recipe Notes:
1. You can adjust the proportion of chili powder to paprika to increase or decrease the spice level.
2. You can substitute chili powder and cumin with harissa seasoning. In this case, use about 1-2 tsp harissa seasoning.
3. If you want it to be spicy, you can add 1-2 finely chopped jalapenos or green chilies in step 2 with onions.
4. You can also use curry powder or garam masala powder instead of or in addition to chili powder.

## My Recipe Notes

**Result:** Loved it ♥   Okay ☑   Not for me ☒
**Spice Level:** Too Spicy 😄   Just Right ☺   Not Spicy Enough 😎
**Date(s):**
**Comments:**

## Spicy Mediterranean Shakshuka Fish #2

This is a little bit different preparation than the previous recipe. Here fish is baked with the shakshuka sauce.

Ingredients
- 4-5 fish filet (Tilapia, Catfish, or your choice fish)
- 1 medium onion, diced
- 3-5 garlic cloves, chopped
- 3 medium tomatoes cut into chunks
- 2 tablespoon extra-virgin olive oil
- ¼ cup cilantro and ¼ cup parsley, chopped
- Salt to taste
- ½ cup pitted, chopped olives
- ½ cup red bell pepper diced into 1-inch chunks
- ½-1 tsp chili powder
- ½ tsp turmeric powder
- 1 tsp cumin powder
- 2-3 tsp paprika
- ½ tsp black pepper powder
- 1-2 tsp lemon juice

Method
1. First marinate fish with salt, ½ tsp chili powder, and ½ tsp turmeric powder, and lemon juice.
2. Heat oil in a non-stick large enough saucepan over medium heat.
3. Add onions and garlic. Sauté until onions become translucent.
4. Add spices.
5. Add tomatoes and bell pepper. Mix well. Cover and cook on low flame for 5-10 minutes or until tomatoes are sufficiently wilted. If needed, stir occasionally so it does not stick to the pan.
6. Now in a non-stick pan add some oil and lightly fry the fish fillets.
7. Once fried, in a large enough baking pan, lay the fried fish side by side.
8. Now add the sauce on top evenly.
9. Bake at 400 degrees for about 20 minutes.
10. Sprinkle black pepper powder, cilantro/parsley, or other herbs (mint, tarragon, chives, or green onions) and serve.

Recipe Notes:
1. You can adjust the proportion of chili powder to paprika to increase or decrease the spice level.
2. You can substitute chili powder and cumin with harissa seasoning. In this case, use about 1-2 tsp harissa seasoning.
3. If you want it to be spicy, you can add 1-2 finely chopped jalapenos or green chilies in step 2 with the onions.
4. You can also use curry powder or garam masala powder instead of or in addition to chili powder.

# My Recipe Notes

**Result:** Loved it ♥   Okay ☑   Not for me ☒

**Spice Level:** Too Spicy 😁   Just Right ☺   Not Spicy Enough 😎

**Date(s):**

**Comments:**

## Spicy Fish with Kimchi

If you are a fan of kimchi and you like fish, this is a very easy recipe to make. This recipe uses canned mackerel. You could also make the same recipe with fresh fish of your choice.

Ingredients
- 2 cans of mackerel
- 4 cups of water
- 1 ½ cup chopped fermented kimchi
- 3-4 garlic cloves crushed
- 1-2 jalapeno pepper sliced diagonally
- 1-2 tsp grated ginger
- 1-2 tbsp Korean hot pepper paste
- 2 stalks celery chopped
- Salt to taste

Method
1. Add kimchi, onions, celery, ginger, garlic, jalapenos, hot pepper sauce, and salt in a large enough pan. Add water and gently mix so pepper sauce and other ingredients are evenly mixed.
2. Bring it to a boil on medium heat.
3. Now add canned mackerel. Pour some of the sauce over the mackerel so that it is fully soaked. Cook for about 10 minutes or until celery is tender and fish is cooked and absorbs the hot pepper and kimchi flavor.

Serve with rice.

Recipe Notes:
1. You can try several variations of this recipe as follows:
    a. Increase the amount of kimchi to 2-3 cups.
    b. Use tuna fish, sardine, or other canned fish instead of mackerel.
    c. If you like to use fresh fish, try cod, salmon, or your choice of fish filet. In this case, you may need a bit more cooking time.
2. You can add green onions (cut into 2-inch pieces), Italian squash, or potato to this preparation.
3. If you like, you can add tofu cut into 1-inch pieces.

# My Recipe Notes

**Result:** Loved it ♥  Okay ☑  Not for me ☒

**Spice Level:** Too Spicy 😁  Just Right ☺  Not Spicy Enough 😎

**Date(s):**

**Comments:**

## Fish in Creamy Cajun Sauce

This is a Louisiana Cajun-style fish recipe. You can adapt this recipe to your taste and spice level.

**Ingredients**
- 2 lbs. catfish filets cut into 2-inch pieces
- 2 tbsp butter
- ½ cup heavy cream
- 1-2 tbsp hot pepper sauce (optional)
- ½ - 1 tsp chili powder
- 2 tbsp Cajun seasoning
- 2 cups of water (or veg/chicken broth)
- 1 medium onion chopped
- 1-2 jalapenos chopped
- 2-3 tomatoes chopped
- 1-2 tsp ginger-garlic paste (optional)
- Salt if required (Cajun seasoning has salt)

Method
1. Heat butter in a large enough pan. Add onions, jalapenos, tomatoes and sauté well until tomatoes break down and onions are cooked.
2. Add chili powder, Cajun seasoning, and optional hot pepper sauce. Stir and cook for another 1 minute.
3. Add water/broth and bring to a boil.
4. Now add fish pieces and heavy cream. Cover and cook for about 10 minutes or until fish is cooked and the sauce is very creamy.

Serve with rice or pasta.

Recipe Notes:
1. You can adjust the proportion of chili powder or hot sauce to increase or decrease the spice level.
2. You can try adding black pepper powder (1-2 tsp) instead of or in addition to chili powder.
3. You can also use curry powder or garam masala powder instead of or in addition to chili powder.
4. You can substitute fish with shrimp if you like.
5. Instead of heavy cream, you can use coconut milk if you prefer.

# My Recipe Notes

**Result:** Loved it ♥   Okay ☑   Not for me ☒

**Spice Level:** Too Spicy 😅   Just Right ☺   Not Spicy Enough 😎

**Date(s):**

**Comments:**

---
---
---
---
---
---
---
---
---
---
---
---
---
---
---
---
---
---
---
---

## Sweet and Spicy Brazilian Fish Stew

This is a Brazilian style fish stew recipe adapted for spice lovers.

**Ingredients**
- 2 lbs. fish filet cut into pieces
- 2 tsp lime juice
- 3 tbsp olive oil
- ½ tsp turmeric powder
- ½ tsp black pepper powder
- ½-1 tsp salt or to taste
- 1 tsp paprika
- 1 tsp cumin powder
- 1-2 tsp brown sugar (optional)
- ½ - 1 tsp cayenne powder
- 1 can coconut milk
- 1 medium onion chopped
- 1 red bell pepper cut into 1-inch pieces
- 2 tomatoes diced
- 1-2 jalapenos chopped (optional)
- 1-2 cups of water/broth
- 5-6 cloves garlic chopped

Method
1. First marinate the fish with lime juice, salt, pepper, turmeric, and 1 tbsp oil. Set aside for 20 minutes in the fridge.
2. In a pan, add 1 tbsp oil and fry the marinated fish for 2 minutes on each side. Drain and set aside.
3. Add test of the oil in the same pan. Sauté onions and garlic. Add spices. Sauté for another 30 seconds – 1 minute.
4. Now add the bell pepper, tomatoes and cook for 3-4 minutes or until tomatoes break down and bell peppers are tender. Add optional sugar.
5. Add coconut milk and some water. Bring to a boil.
6. Now add fish pieces. Cover and simmer for 3-4 minutes or until fish is fully coated with sauce.

Serve with rice or pasta.

Recipe Notes:
1. You can adjust the proportion of chili powder to increase or decrease the spice level. If you want more color but less heat, use Kashmiri chili powder.
2. You can also use curry powder or garam masala powder instead of or in addition to chili powder.
3. You can substitute fish with shrimp if you like.
4. In addition to red bell pepper, you could also add green bell pepper or Italian squash.
5. You could also puree onions, garlic, and tomatoes first and then sauté in oil instead of sautéing cut pieces. This will make the dish more creamy.
6. You can also add shrimp along with fish pieces in this recipe.

7. Sugar is optional. Instead of adding sugar, you can also add chopped red/yellow sweet peppers, which will provide color and sweetness.

Notes:

## My Recipe Notes

**Result:** Loved it ♥    Okay ☑    Not for me ☒

**Spice Level:** Too Spicy 😁    Just Right 🙂    Not Spicy Enough 😎

**Date(s):**

**Comments:**

## INSTANT POT SPICY SPANISH SEAFOOD STEW

This is a quick and easy Spanish seafood stew in an instant pot.

**Ingredients**
- 2 filets of fresh/frozen code cut up
- ½ lbs. large shrimp peeled and deveined
- 10 mussels cleaned and washed
- ½ tsp turmeric powder
- ½ tsp black pepper powder
- 1 tsp cumin powder
- 1 - 2 tsp Spanish paprika
- 1 medium onion chopped
- 1 can of diced tomatoes
- 1-2 jalapenos chopped (optional)
- ¼ cup white wine (optional)
- 1-2 cups of water/broth
- 5-6 cloves garlic chopped

Method
1. With the instant pot set to sauté, cook onions, garlic, jalapenos.
2. Add spices. Sauté for another 30 seconds – 1 minute.
3. Now add tomatoes, wine, and mix until well combined.
4. Add cleaned mussels, shrimp, and fish pieces and mix gently so the fish is well coated.
5. Change the setting to manual and cook for 3-4 minutes under high pressure.
6. Release steam immediately.

Garnish with cilantro and serve.

# My Recipe Notes

**Result:** Loved it ♥   Okay ☑   Not for me ☒

**Spice Level:** Too Spicy 😁   Just Right ☺   Not Spicy Enough 😎

**Date(s):**

**Comments:**

## Spicy Herb Baked Fish

Ingredients
- 2 whole fish scaled and cleaned
- ½ tsp pepper powder (optional)
- 3-6 cloves of garlic peeled
- 1-inch piece of ginger peeled
- 1-3 jalapenos chopped
- 1 cup cilantro
- 1 cup dill
- 1 cup mint
- 1-2 tsp lime juice
- 2 tbsp olive oil
- 1 tsp salt

Method
1. Make cuts on both sides of the fish evenly so the herbs can be applied before baking.
2. Grind herbs, ginger, garlic, jalapenos and make a paste. Add salt, olive oil, and lime juice and mix well.
3. Apply the herb paste on the cuts made into the fish as well as inside the cleaned fish.
4. Wrap the fish in banana leaves, bamboo leaves, or grape leaves tightly. Use kitchen twine to tie or use an aluminum foil to seal further.
5. Cook on an open flame, grill, or bake in the oven.

Recipe Notes:
1. Usually, 1 or 2 jalapenos should give enough heat. Use more jalapenos if you like it spicy.
2. You can use other herbs such as basil, thyme, parsley, or chives in the preparations. Use the ones you like, try different combinations.
3. If you are cooking on an open fire, you may need extra layers of banana leaves to wrap the fish.

# My Recipe Notes

**Result:** Loved it ♥   Okay ☑   Not for me ☒

**Spice Level:** Too Spicy 😅   Just Right 🙂   Not Spicy Enough 😎

**Date(s):**

**Comments:**

## Spicy Mediterranean Baked Fish

This recipe is like the shakshuka recipe earlier. This recipe uses capers instead of olives. The preparation is pretty much similar.

Ingredients
- 4-5 fish filet (Tilapia, Catfish, or your choice fish)
- 1 medium onion, diced
- 8-10 garlic cloves, chopped
- 3 medium tomatoes cut into chunks
- 2 tablespoon extra-virgin olive oil
- ¼ cup cilantro and ¼ cup parsley, chopped
- Salt to taste
- ½ cup capers
- ½ cup red bell pepper diced into 1-inch chunks
- 1 tsp coriander powder
- 1 tsp cumin powder
- 2-3 tsp paprika
- ½ tsp black pepper powder
- 2-4 Jalapeno slit (optional)
- 1-2 tsp lemon juice
- 2 tbsp olive oil
-

Method
1. First marinate fish with salt, black pepper powder, and lemon juice.
2. Heat olive oil in a non-stick large enough saucepan over medium heat.
3. Add onions and garlic. Sauté until onions become translucent.
4. Add spices.
5. Add tomatoes, bell pepper, and optional jalapenos. Mix well. Cover and cook on low flame for 5-10 minutes or until tomatoes are sufficiently wilted. If needed, stir occasionally so it does not stick to the pan.
6. In a large enough baking pan, spread some of the sauce from the previous step. Now arrange the fish filets and top it with the rest of the sauce.
7. Bake at 400 degrees for about 20 minutes.
8. Sprinkle cilantro/parsley or other herbs (mint, tarragon, chives, or green onions) and serve with lemon slices over rice.

Recipe Notes:
1. You can adjust paprika to increase or decrease the spice level.
2. You can substitute chili powder and cumin with harissa seasoning. In this case, use about 1-2 tsp harissa seasoning.
3. If you want it to be spicy, you can add 1-2 finely chopped jalapenos or green chilies. Add them in step 2 with onions.
4. Instead of a fish filet, you can use cleaned whole fish. In this case, fry the marinated fish in oil before baking. You may also need to bake for an extra 5 minutes.

# My Recipe Notes

**Result:** Loved it ♥   Okay ☑   Not for me ☒
**Spice Level:** Too Spicy 😆   Just Right ☺   Not Spicy Enough 😎
**Date(s):**
**Comments:**

## SRI LANKAN FISH CURRY

Sri Lanka is an island nation in the Indian ocean. Though Sri Lanka has a distinct cuisine, due to its physical proximity to South India, many recipes are very close to some of the south Indian recipes.

Because Sri Lanka is an island nation, fish is plently available and most people eat fish. Rice and fish are comfort food for Sri Lankans.

Though there are variations in recipes, a basic Sri Lankan fish curry is made with coconut milk, onions, ginger, garlic and sliced tomatoes, in addition to aromatic and healthy spice combinations (chili powder, turmeric, cloves, nutmeg, cinnamon, black pepper, fenugreek, cumin, coriander, and others). Usually, tamarind paste is added to provide the sourness or acidity, but some preparations use the "black tamarind" or dried Garcinia Cambogia. Both are available in most Asian stores.

**Ingredients**
- 2 lbs. salmon filet cut into pieces.
- coconut oil – 2 tbsp
- ½ tsp mustard seeds
- ½ tsp Fenugreek seeds
- 1 medium onion chopped
- 1 tsp ginger paste
- 1 tsp garlic paste
- Tamarind paste/pulp - 2 tsp
- 1 tsp curry powder
- ½ tsp turmeric powder
- 1-2 tsp chili powder
- 1 can coconut milk
- Salt to taste
- 1 spring curry leaves
- 2-4 sliced green chilies or jalapeños, seeds removed (optional)

Method
1. Heat oil in a deep bottom pan, add oil, crackle mustard seeds. While mustard seeds are crackling, add fenugreek seeds and curry leaves (curry leaves could cause oil to splatter so be careful).
2. Add onions, green chilies, ginger, and garlic paste. Sauté for about a minute or until onion becomes translucent. Add spices. Mix well.
3. Add coconut milk and tamarind. Mix well and bring to a boil.
4. Add cut and washed salmon pieces. Gently swirl the pot or use a spoon to mix gently (so the fish does not break) so the fish is fully covered with the sauce. Cook covered for about 5-10 minutes or until the fish is cooked well.

Serve with rice.

There are many variations to Sri Lankan fish curry. See the notes below to try different variations and make your own special recipe.

Recipe Notes:
1. In many Sri Lankan recipes, cinnamon sticks (Sri Lanka is one of the largest exporters of cinnamon) and cardamom are added. Adding these will provide a more distinct flavor and aroma.

2. Instead of tamarind or in addition to tamarind, you may also add kokum or the black tamarind.
3. You can also add tomatoes if you like in this recipe.
4. You can get Sri Lankan curry powder in Asian stores and may be used instead of standard curry powder.
5. In some preparations, fennel is added along with the rest of the spices.

Notes:

## My Recipe Notes

**Result:** Loved it ♥   Okay ☑   Not for me ☒
**Spice Level:** Too Spicy 😁   Just Right ☺   Not Spicy Enough 😎
**Date(s):**
**Comments:**

---------------------------------------------------------
---------------------------------------------------------
---------------------------------------------------------
---------------------------------------------------------
---------------------------------------------------------
---------------------------------------------------------
---------------------------------------------------------
---------------------------------------------------------
---------------------------------------------------------
---------------------------------------------------------
---------------------------------------------------------
---------------------------------------------------------
---------------------------------------------------------
---------------------------------------------------------
---------------------------------------------------------
---------------------------------------------------------
---------------------------------------------------------
---------------------------------------------------------
---------------------------------------------------------

## SPICY SALMON WITH COCONUT SAUCE

This is a very quick and delightful recipe and is closer to Mediterranean style than an Asian fish recipe.

**Ingredients**
- two 6 oz salmon filet, washed (skin on/off)
- 1 tbsp butter
- 1 tsp ginger paste
- 1 tsp garlic paste
- ½ of medium onion chopped
- 1 medium tomato chopped up
- ¼ tsp pepper powder
- 2 tsp lemon juice
- ½ tsp chili powder
- ½ tsp curry powder (optional)
- ½ can coconut milk
- Salt to taste

Method
1. Sprinkle salt and pepper on both sides of the salmon and set aside for 10 minutes.
2. Melt butter and fry salmon on both sides in butter basting on all sides with melted butter. Once cooked, pour the lemon juice on top and set aside.
3. Sauté onions in the same pan, add ginger, garlic, and spices and mix for a couple of minutes until spice is aromatic. Add coconut milk keep cooking until sauce is thickened.
4. Plate the fried salmon and pour sauce on top of it. Garnish with an herb of your choice (cilantro, basil, parsley) and serve.

You can try several variations as per the notes below.

Recipe Notes:
1. You can add 2 tablespoons of tomato puree in step 3.
2. You can puree the sautéed onion at the end of step 3 and use the pureed sauce for the rest of the recipe steps.
3. You can make an herb sauce by adding cilantro and/or mint in step 3 and making a puree out of it.

# My Recipe Notes

**Result:** Loved it ♥   Okay ☑   Not for me ☒

**Spice Level:** Too Spicy 😄   Just Right 🙂   Not Spicy Enough 😎

**Date(s):**

**Comments:**

## Easy Thai Red Curry with Fish

Ingredients
- 1 lb. salmon filet, cut into 1-inch pieces
- 1 tbsp coconut oil
- 1 tbsp ginger-garlic paste
- 2 tomatoes sliced
- ¼ cup or 4 tbsp red curry paste
- 2 cans of coconut milk
- ¼ cup Thai basil chopped
- ½ inch piece of ginger
- 2 lime leaves

Method
1. Heat oil in a large pan over medium heat, sauté ginger-garlic paste for about a minute. Add tomatoes and Thai red curry paste and mix for another minute.
2. Add coconut milk and bring it to a boil.
3. Add fish pieces and lime leaves. Bring to a boil and simmer covered for 10-15 minutes or until fish is cooked.
4. Add Thai basil. Mix. Switch off the heat. Keep it covered for a couple of minutes before serving.

## My Recipe Notes

**Result:** Loved it ♥   Okay ☑   Not for me ☒

**Spice Level:** Too Spicy 😆   Just Right ☺   Not Spicy Enough 😎

**Date(s):**

**Comments:**

## SPICY MEDITERRANEAN-INDIAN-THAI FISH

This recipe is a fusion of Mediterranean, Indian, and Thai style ingredients. This is quick to make and is healthy.

Ingredients
- 4-6 pieces of salmon 6 oz (170 gm) each
- ¼ cup extra virgin olive oil
- 1 tbsp ginger grated
- 1 tbsp garlic finely chopped
- 2 tbsp Thai red curry paste
- 2 tsp Thai fish sauce
- ½ tsp turmeric powder
- ¼ tsp black pepper powder
- 1 can (2 cups) of coconut milk
- ¼ cilantro chopped
- 2 tbsp lemongrass chopped
- Salt to taste
- 1 tbsp lime juice
- 1 lime sliced (optional)

Method
1. Sprinkle, ¼ tsp salt, turmeric, and pepper on the salmon filet on both sides and set aside for 10 minutes.
2. Heat oil in a large pan over medium heat, fry salmon on both sides – about 1-2 minutes each side. Remove the salmon and set aside.
3. In the same pan, add ginger, garlic to the oil. Sauté for about a minute. Now add lemongrass, Thai red curry paste, and fish sauce. Sauté well. Add coconut milk and bring to a boil.
4. Add fish pieces and lime slices. Pour some of the spicy coconut sauce on top of the fish so it gets soaked. Simmer it for about 5 minutes covered.
5. Garnish with fresh cilantro and serve.

# My Recipe Notes

**Result:** Loved it ♥    Okay ☑    Not for me ☒
**Spice Level:** Too Spicy 😅    Just Right ☺    Not Spicy Enough 😎
**Date(s):**
**Comments:**

## Spicy Louisiana Fish Fry

This is a Louisiana Cajun-style fish fry but with added spices for the spice lovers. You can adapt this recipe to your taste and spice level if chose to.

**Ingredients**
- 2 lbs. catfish filets cut into 2-inch pieces
- ¼ - ½ cup oil for frying
- 1-2 tsp ginger-garlic paste
- 1-2 tbsp hot pepper sauce (optional)
- ½ - 1 tsp chili powder
- 2 - 3 tsp black pepper powder
- 1 egg
- 2 tbsp Cajun seasoning
- ½ cup of all-purpose flour
- ¼ cup of cornmeal

Method
1. Beat eggs in a bowl. Add chili powder, hot pepper sauce, ginger-garlic paste and mix well, and set aside.
2. Mix Cajun seasoning, chili powder, cornmeal, all-purpose flour, cornmeal, and black pepper powder to create a dry mix.
3. Dip fish pieces in dry mixture and then into the whisked egg-ginger-garlic-hot sauce mixture and then back to the dry mixture so fish pieces are well coated with the seasoning. Set it aside in the fridge for 15-30 minutes so the batter sticks to fish well.
4. Heat oil in a pan on medium-high heat. Fry the fish on each side for about 2-3 minutes so the fish is cooked, and the batter is golden brown.
5. Remove fried fish pieces and drain them on a paper towel.

Serve with your choice of sauce (tomato ketchup, tartar sauce, or hot sauce)

# My Recipe Notes

**Result:** Loved it ♥  Okay ☑  Not for me ☒
**Spice Level:** Too Spicy 😄  Just Right ☺  Not Spicy Enough 😎
**Date(s):**
**Comments:**

_____
_____
_____
_____
_____
_____
_____
_____
_____
_____
_____
_____
_____
_____
_____
_____
_____
_____
_____
_____
_____

## Spicy Grilled Fish in Coconut Sauce (Samaki Wa Kupaka)

Samaki wa kupaka is an African (originally Tanzanian) dish that is made from whole grilled fish in coconut sauce.

**Ingredients**
- 2 medium size (6-10 inches) whole fish cleaned

For the marinade
- ½ - 1 tsp chili powder
- ½ tsp turmeric powder
- 1 tsp coriander powder
- 1 tsp garlic paste
- 1 tsp ginger paste
- 4 tbsp lemon juice
- Salt to taste

For the coconut sauce
- 1 cup fresh grated coconut
- 1-2 green chilies
- 1 tomato sliced
- 2 tbsp tomato paste
- 1 tsp turmeric powder
- 1 tsp ginger-garlic paste
- Salt to taste

Method
1. First, make cuts into the fish at regular intervals (½ inch apart) on both sides of the fish.
2. Combine all the ingredients for the marinade and apply the marinade on both sides of the fish. Set aside for 20 minutes.
3. Meanwhile, you can make coconut sauce by blending all the items for coconut sauce to make a puree in a blender.
4. Cook the sauce in a pan on low heat so that the sauce gets cooked and become thick and set aside.
5. Grill the fish in an open grill or the oven.
6. Once grilled, apply the coconut sauce on both sides of the fish and serve.

Recipe Notes:
1. After applying coconut sauce in step 6 above, the fish may be returned to the oven/grill to cook some more with the coconut sauce, if you like.
2. Instead of fresh coconut, you could use a can of store-bought coconut milk.
3. You can make the coconut sauce by combining coconut milk, 1 cup tamarind juice, 1 tsp chili powder, 1 tsp turmeric, and 1 tsp ginger-garlic paste. In this case, simply combine them.
4. You can garnish the fish with chopped up cilantro or parsley before serving.
5. Instead of whole fish, you could cut the fish, marinate, and fry them in oil and serve with coconut sauce.

6. While the traditional dish uses coconut-based sauce, you could try a tomato-based sauce. In this case, instead of coconut, you puree tomatoes and other ingredients to make the sauce.

Notes:

## My Recipe Notes

**Result:** Loved it ♥   Okay ☑   Not for me ☒
**Spice Level:** Too Spicy 😅   Just Right 🙂   Not Spicy Enough 😎
**Date(s):**
**Comments:**

## FINAL NOTES AND GENERAL TIPS FOR COOKING SPICY FISH

1. Fish cooks faster than other proteins. There is a 10-minute rule for cooking fish which states for every 1 inch in thickness of the fish, cook for 10 minutes. This means if your fish steak is 1 inch thick and you are grilling, frying, or baking, cook both sides for about 5 minutes. The internal temperature should reach 145 degrees (C) and should be able to flake the fish with a fork.
2. The spices you can use with fish is limited by your creativity and imagination. Mix and match the spices as you like. Chili powder, turmeric, and black pepper powder goes well with shrimp. Other spices or spice mixes can be used according to your taste.
3. I have used turmeric, ginger, and garlic in most of the recipes. In my opinion, these three spices are fundamental and offer a lot of healing power and make the dish very healthy. I have written separate books on these spices as they are so important in healthy food preparations.
4. Fish generates water while cooking. So, if you like your dish to be dry and not saucy, you may want to pat down the fish before cooking.
5. If you are adding vegetables to fish, cook them first so that it becomes tender before adding fish. This is true when using fish with other ingredients as well. Add fish mostly towards the end of cooking.
6. While I have described most recipes as using fish filets, if you prefer, you can use fish with bones. You can also use the fish head in some of these recipes, especially the grilling, baking, or curry recipes.
7. If you are frying fish first as given in some of the recipes, turn them over after 5 minutes on each side (see note 1 above).
8. If you are currying fish, after cooking, you may want to keep it in the sauce for 30 minutes or more for the fish to absorb the flavor, acidity, and spices.
9. For the sourness or acidity of the spicy fish, use one or more of the following:
    - Tamarind or tamarind paste
    - Kokum
    - Black Tamarind/Garcinia Combogia
    - Fresh Tomatoes or tomato paste
    - Lemon Juice
    - Kimchi
    - Vinegar
10. The following are the usual spices that are used in fish preparations
    - Chili powder
    - Coriander Powder
    - Cumin Powder
    - Turmeric Powder
    - Green Chilies
    - Jalapenos
    - Black pepper powder
11. You can use one or more of the following spice mixes
    - Curry Powder (any kind)
    - Garam masala
    - Thai red curry paste

12. Following are some of the other ingredients used in spicy fish preparations.
    - Ginger
    - Garlic
    - Fenugreek
    - Mustard seeds
    - Curry leaves
    - Coriander leaves/Cilantro
    - Mint
    - Basil leaves
    - Onions

Notes:

Notes:

# Additional Notes & Observations on the Recipes

**My favorite places to buy spices:**

**My favorite spice and why**

**Comments:**

## My Favorite Fish Recipe

**Write down or paste your favorite curry recipe below:**

# My Family Recipe

Source: Mom  Dad  Grandma  Grandpa  Other:
Write down or paste your family recipe below:

## DISCLAIMER

This book details the author's personal experiences in using Indian spices, the information contained in the public domain as well as the author's opinion. The author is not licensed as a doctor, nutritionist, or chef. The author is providing this book and its contents on an "as is" basis and makes no representations or warranties of any kind with respect to this book or its contents. The author disclaims all such representations and warranties, including for example warranties of merchantability and educational or medical advice for a particular purpose. In addition, the author does not represent or warrant that the information accessible via this book is accurate, complete, or current. The statements made about products and services have not been evaluated by the US FDA or any equivalent organization in other countries.

The author will not be liable for damages arising out of or in connection with the use of this book or the information contained within. This is a comprehensive limitation of liability that applies to all damages of any kind, including (without limitation) compensatory; direct, indirect, or consequential damages; loss of data, income, or profit; loss of or damage to property, and claims of third parties. It is understood that this book is not intended as a substitute for consultation with a licensed medical or a culinary professional. Before starting any lifestyle changes, it is recommended that you consult a licensed professional to ensure that you are doing what is best for your situation. The use of this book implies your acceptance of this disclaimer.

## Thank You

If you enjoyed this book or found it useful, I would greatly appreciate, if you could post a short review. I read all the reviews and your feedback will help me to make this book even better.

## About the Author

Joseph Veebe is passionate about a healthy lifestyle. Veebe believes many modern sickness and health conditions are due to unhealthy eating habits and poor lifestyle. His books are a result of his research into healthy living and his experiments in the kitchen where he loves to cook healthy food with fresh ingredients for his family.

Veebe understands that most people do not have enough time in their busy days for elaborate home cooking. So, it is essential to simplify the cooking process. His recipes follow an 80-20 rule. 80% of authentic taste and flavor with 20% effort and time compared to elaborate or authentic recipes. All his recipes use fresh ingredients. He avoids processed foods like a plague and believes processed foods have too many harmful chemicals that are not good for long term consumption.

Most people do not want to spend too much time in the kitchen to cook up elaborate and prescriptive recipes. Veebe hopes that his recipes will save time & money, help people make healthy choices, and inspire them to experiment while preparing healthy, natural, and delicious food for the family. Almost all Veebe's recipes use natural ingredients such as superfoods, spices, and herbs that are proven to have many health benefits. Veebe's recipes are meant for everyday cooking.

He started writing these books as healthy living notes and recipes to benefit his daughters someday. Veebe hopes others find these books helpful as well. Visit www.essentialhealthandwellness.net for more information.

## COOKING MEASUREMENTS AND CONVERSION CHARTS

Some of you may be using a different kitchen measurement system than described in the book. I believe most people can navigate these different systems. The following conversion tables included as a ready reference; in case you need it.

| US Dry Volume Measurements ||
|---|---|
| **Measurement** | **Equivalent** |
| 3 teaspoons | 1 Tablespoon |
| ¼ cup | 4 Tablespoons |
| 1/3 cup | 5 1/3 Tablespoons |
| ½ cup | 8 Tablespoons |
| ¾ cup | 12 Tablespoons |
| 1 cup | 16 Tablespoons |
| 1 Pound | 16 ounces |

| US Liquid Volume Measurements and Conversion ||
|---|---|
| 8 Fluid ounces | 1 Cup |
| 1 Pint | 2 Cups (or 16 fluid ounces) |
| 1 Quart | 2 Pints (or 4 cups) |
| 1 Gallon | 4 Quarts (or 16 cups) |

| US to Metric Conversions ||
|---|---|
| 1 teaspoon | 5 ml |
| 1 tablespoon | 15 ml |
| 1 fluid oz. | 30 ml |
| 1 cup | 240 ml |
| 2 cups (1 pint) | 470 ml |
| 4 cups (1 quart) | 940 ml or approx. 1 litre |
| 4 quarts (1 gal.) | 3.8 liters or 16 cups |
| 1 oz. | 28 grams |
| 1 pound (16 Oz.) | 454 grams or approx. ½ kilo gram |

| Metric to US Conversions ||
|---|---|
| 100 ml | 3.4 fluid oz. |
| 240 ml | 1 cup |

| | |
|---|---|
| 1 liter | 34 fluid oz./ 4.2 cups/2.1 Pints/1.06 quarts/0.26 gallon |
| 100 grams | 3.5 ounces |
| 500 grams | 1.10 pounds |
| 1 kilogram | 2.205 pounds or 35 oz. |

| Oven Temperature Conversions | |
|---|---|
| Fahrenheit | Celsius |
| 275º F | 140º C |
| 300º F | 150º C |
| 325º F | 165º C |
| 350º F | 180º C |
| 375º F | 190º C |
| 400º F | 200º C |
| 425º F | 220º C |
| 450º F | 230º C |
| 475º F | 240º C |

Printed in Great Britain
by Amazon